RANDALL'S RULES

The Definitive Guide For Successfully Navigating The Coaching Profession

VOLUME ONE

COACH MORGAN RANDALL

LEGAL NOTICE EVEN COACHES DARE NOT IGNORE!

Coach Morgan Randall

Randall's Rules volume one

Copyright © 2018 by Coach Morgan Randall

All rights reserved. No part of this book may be reproduced or transmitted in any for or by any means, electronic or mechanical, including photocopying, recording or by any information storage and retrieval system, without express written permission from the publisher, except for the inclusion of brief quotations in critical articles or a review.

Because this book is an entertainment product, it is not a substitute for professional advice on the topics discussed in it.

You are advised to do your own due diligence when it comes to making any decisions. Use caution and seek the advice of qualified professionals before acting upon the contents of this book. You shall not consider any examples, documents or other content in this book or otherwise provided by the author or publisher to be the equivalent of professional advice. The author and publisher assume no responsibility for any loses or damages resulting from your use of any information contained in this book.

Request for permission should be made in writing or online to:

    Coach Morgan Randall

    Radnor University

    www.CoachMorganRandall.com

    info@CoachMorganRandall.com

Library of Congress Control Number: 2018966898

ISBN: 978-0-9850671-6-8

Printed in the United States of America

PRAISE AND SHAMELESS SELF-PROMOTION FOR RANDALL'S RULES

"So good I can't decide whether it makes me want to rap or meditate."
-Tupac Chopra

"Coach Randall walks a fine line between genius and senility."
-Mason Dixon

"His writing is colorful and it's a real time saver."
-Red Hour-Back

"I bought this book for my boyfriend Ken and he loved it."
-Barb E. Dahl

"The travel tips were most helpful."
-Bonnie Ann Clyde

"I'm only endorsing this because I felt sorry for him."
-Charity Case

"Reading this will put you to sleep."
-Constance Noring

"This book makes a great gift for under the Christmas tree."
-Douglas Furr

RANDALL'S RULES VOLUME ONE

"Randall's will dramatically improve the direction your program is headed."
-Easton West

"A complete 180 from his last book."
Weston East

"If I were grading Randall's Rules, I'd give it an A plus."
-Hy Marx

"Everything I read really rings true."
-Isadore Bell

"A timeless classic, his old school approach will take you back to how things were done decades ago."
-Gerry Atrick

"I'm glad I found this when I did."
-Justin Time

"I was Coach Randall's editor and boy was he a pain in the rear to work with."
-Lance Butz

"Randall's rules is a great recipe for success."
-Amelia Cook

"If you're a Division Three coach Randall's Rules will help you make more money."
-Lois Turner

"Randall's Rules is guaranteed to amplify your voice on campus."
-Mike Raffone

"So good you'll read it cover to cover in one sitting."
-Paige Turner

"You're going to want to keep a pen and paper handy."
-Reid Enright

"This is my favorite of all Coach Randall's books in the participation trophy series."
-Stan Lee Cupp

"It was so good I can't wait to read the sequel."
-Tad Moore

"I guarantee Randall's Rules helps take your program to the next level."
-Will Wynn

"If you program is underfunded, THIS is the book for you."
-Owen Cash

DEDICATION

This book is dedicated to you. I want you to avoid the mistakes, bumps, bruises and embarrassments I've experienced over the years in my travels.

ACKNOWLEDGMENTS

Special thanks to everyone who didn't endorse this book.

INTRODUCTION

Thank you for investing in volume one of Randall's Rules. This resource is comprised of hard learned lessons that are a testament to the occupational hazard that comes with the territory of being a road warrior.

With that said, hopefully you already know some of the hazards come with the territory. This book will help you avoid the other ones. You're probably wondering how I might know about all of these. Quite simply, I've made every mistake in the book. At least twice. So, hopefully I will help you avoid many of the dangers and frustrations of life on the road as a coach and world-class recruiter.

*Disclaimer: These rules are not a substitute for advice or consultation with a physician, dietician, psychologist, psychiatrist or any other type of medical professional whose job title ends in "cian" or "ist".

RULE #1
NEVER UNPACK YOUR BAG

This is the very first rule for a very good reason. Coaching and recruiting involves a ton of travel. On these journeys you will encounter quite a few bizarre, not so safe, awkward and occasionally downright dangerous situations on the road. *(Like in 1996 when the Smithtown Motor Lodge had a Cadillac in the parking lot with bullet holes in the windshield and the motel advertised an hourly rate not a nightly rate. That's another story for another book though.)*

I know it's tempting to put your clothes in the drawers of the hotel dresser when you're on the road and away from the comforts of home. Trust me this is a huge mistake. The last thing you want to do is have to repack all your stuff in the morning when you miss the wake-up call, oversleep and have five minutes to get to the bus before the team and the rest of the coaching staff are tempted to leave without you. You also don't want to forget your clothes in the hotel dresser. This comes in especially handy when you need to make a quick escape from a girl (or guy) you hooked up with who came back to your hotel room and won't leave. Always keep your bag packed, ready to bolt at a moment's notice.

RULE #2

ALWAYS KEEP A SPARE BAG PACKED

In other words, carry an extra dress shirt, tie and pair of pants in the trunk of your car. If you don't, you'll wish you did when you spill a bacon double cheese burrito all over your shirt after going through the drive thru on your way to that home visit of your top recruit. *(Yeah I did that)* If you iron the spare clothes and carefully fold them in a shirt box you won't need to iron the shirt again before wearing it. Invest in a good garment folder on Amazon, you'll thank me later.

RULE #3

PRESS YOUR TONGUE AGAINST THE ROOF OF YOUR MOUTH IF YOU HAVE BRAIN FREEZE.

(Just thought you ought to know this.)

RULE #4

KEEP A LINT ROLLER IN YOUR CAR OR TRAVEL BAG

They're basically the poor man's dry cleaning service. While it might not get the shirt clean, it will at least make the shirt LOOK clean.

(Division I coaches don't have to worry about this rule, they can actually afford dry cleaning.)

RULE #5

EXPECT NOTHING AND YOU'LL NEVER BE DISAPPOINTED

I'm not trying to rain on your parade, okay maybe a little bit but it's for a good reason. You need to have realistic expectations. I remember all too well the days of making in home visits thinking "this blue chip prospect slipped through the cracks and we have a great shot at signing him". I thought "this will be the one who turns our fortunes around and now we will get a pipeline into this program and sign other great players in subsequent years". Only to have some mid-major program swoop in late in the process and scoop the kid up and have my hopes and dreams shattered.

I probably should have made this rule number one. The reason this rule is so important is because your ability to stick to this rule throughout your coaching career will determine how long you'll be able to maintain your sanity and maintain a career in coaching before your brain (or your athletic director) tell you to quit.

Don't get me wrong you should definitely be excited to be recruiting, after all it's the life blood of your program. But what you can't do is put all your eggs in one basket, hang your hopes on one prospect, all your faith in one high school coach or your dreams of a championship in one recruiting class. Some high school or travel team coaches will tell you how they're advising a kid to come to your school and that he's pushing their parents to have the kid sign with you. But when signing day rolls around something mysteriously changes. Don't let situations like this discourage you. A career as a coach and recruiter is a marathon not a sprint. Your career won't last very long if you treat it like it's the 40 yard dash.

RULE #6

TURN ON THE HEATED SEAT IN YOUR CAR TO KEEP PIZZA HOT WHILE YOU DRIVE HOME.

RULE #7
ALWAYS EXPECT EVERYTHING!

After reading rule number five I know it sounds like I'm contradicting myself but follow me on this.

As coaches we get what we expect, so we should expect everything from the support staff, assistant coaches on our campus and the players on our roster. As a species, sports information directors, athletic trainers, compliance officers and facility managers are notoriously lazy and love to pretend they are busy by hiding behind their computer screens whining about all the imaginary work they have piling up.

They focus on whatever sport is in season and whichever coach they fear the most. Often times they will just yes you to death to keep you from going over their head to hold them accountable. You should hold each and every one of them accountable and make sure they're working just as hard for your program as you are. You and your assistant coaches should also be working hard not just with one another, but for one another. (There's a big difference) This means eating healthy, getting enough sleep and exercise as well as staying away from excessive amounts of alcohol.

You should set goals and establish a strong work ethic with high expectations for everyone involved in your program. If support staff, players or assistants fall short of meeting these expectations there should be consequences. This might even involve replacing them. Remember how I told you in rule number five that coaching is a marathon not a sprint? Marathons are won by the well trained and highly conditioned. Hold yourself to a higher standard than everyone else on and off the field because people don't follow what you say, they follow what you do. And it's the right thing to do.

RULE #8
GET OUT OF DODGE FAST

This rule isn't important until you need it to be. It's kind of like the difference between a fire plan and a fire drill. A fire plan is all theory, a memo that gets handed out once a year (and promptly thrown away without being read). A fire drill is an exit strategy that you practice on a regular basis. This rule is about always planning your way out of a facility. Rule #8 applies more to gyms, stadiums and arenas than hotels but you need to know your way out of wherever you are. It's all about having an out. This rule refers to the fact that as a team you've got to have your equipment pretty self-contained and in close proximity to you for when you need to make a quick exit of the facility.

On some occasions you will be at a multi-team tournament. And unless you're the very last game of the day, there will be teams leaving the field before you and taking the field right after you. Nothing pisses off other coaches quite like a team from a prior game taking entirely too long to get on or off the field. Most tournament games don't start or end on time, which means everyone is in a rush. You want to have your equipment and bags located in a place where they are easy to get to as you're coming on and off the field.

Ex. Player equipment bags lined up numerically right behind your bench.

The ability to get in and out of the facility quickly is strong display of your team's professionalism and attention to detail. If you have fans waiting to get autographs or heaven forbid helicopter parents waiting to tell their kid how well they played and tell you how you're not utilizing all their talents correctly, direct them to a designated tailgating area off the field so they're not in the way because you know they weren't going to help pack up anyway.

RULE #9

IF YOU DON'T HAVE A MICROWAVE IN YOUR OFFICE, YOU CAN WARM UP A SANDWICH BY PLACING IT BETWEEN TWO LAP TOP CHARGERS.

RULE #10

NEVER TRUST THE BUSINESS MANAGER

Whether they work in your athletic department or across campus in the business office, they are not your friend. They are glorified criminals and your mortal enemy. Their only focus is on pinching every penny humanly possible. And they make it their mission is to get three nickels from every dime.

They will find every way possible to screw you over. Keep a close eye on your fundraising account to keep an accurate count of how much money your team has raised and make sure it matches the balance in your account. If you can't access that information online on your own, set an alert in your calendar to request a report showing your balance every single week. Business managers will change the numbers and rob Peter to pay Paul as often as they can get away with it. It would be irresponsible of you not to check, double check and triple check to make sure funds raised and your account balance match up correctly.

Back in the 1980's our business manager at Radnor University was also the men's basketball coach. (Red flag #1) He spent money like a drunk politician in Vegas and when his budget was depleted, he magically transferred $20,000 out of my fundraising account to pay for having the basketball court renovated. When that wasn't enough money he took a thousand dollars out of every other team's fundraising account to make up the difference. And no, he was never disciplined in any way, shape or form for stealing from his colleagues. Or should I say he wasn't disciplined by the institution. I made sure I found a way to pay him back though by teaching my players a short cut from the field to the locker room (across the basketball court in their cleats).

Basically, never trust anyone who has a calculator sitting on their desk.

RULE #11

NEVER KEEP THE MEAL MONEY AND ALCOHOL IN THE SAME PLACE

(Keep in mind, I wrote this rule back in 1920 when Prohibition began but it still makes sense today. And yes I am that old.)

It's best not to travel with beer or liquor when travelling with students of any age. But, if you do, a gym bag with a large stack of cash and bottles of liquor will give the appearance of bootlegging or selling to underage people. It will get both the alcohol and the cash confiscated and potentially have charges pressed against whoever claims the gym bag as theirs. The sports information director usually makes a great fall guy for this as he pretty much hates everybody.

RULE #12

IF YOU DON'T HAVE A MICROWAVE IN YOUR HOTEL ROOM, YOU CAN HEAT UP A SANDWICH OR SLICE OF PIZZA ON THE IRON. TO HEAT IT TWICE AS FAST, BLOW THE HAIR DRYER ON THE TOP OF THE PIZZA TOO.

RULE #13
STASH YOUR CASH

Keep your meal money in a safe hiding place in case the bus is robbed, searched or broken into. Same rule applies to hotel rooms. I took my team to Orlando for a spring break tournament. While we were at practice, the housekeepers keyed into every one of our rooms and stole all my players' cash out of their wallets. The hotel refused to accept responsibility even though in addition to video surveillance camera footage, there is also a computer record of who keys into each room and at precisely what time. (Remember this next time you travel.)

Long story short, I called the police and in lieu of me pressing charges they negotiated with the hotel to reimburse my players for the cash that was stolen. I of course encouraged each my players to generously overestimate how much money was taken.

Note: This situation did not impact me for two reasons:

1. I'm a small college coach so I never have much money.

2. I followed Rule #13.

RULE #14
BECOME A MINIMALIST

This rule goes hand in hand with rule number one.

Limit yourself to packing just one small bag or backpack. Only pack the essentials because the more you pack, the more there is to possibly get lost or left behind at the stadium, locker room or hotel room.

Also, the last thing you want to have to do is schlep 50 lbs. of baggage and equipment through the airport. If you do, your coach and institution will hate you because it now costs a small fortune to check baggage on commercial flights.

(Everyone reading this who isn't a Division One coach is laughing at that last sentence and thinking… air travel… What's that?)

RULE #15

EGGS ARE EXTREMELY HEALTHY, A GREAT SOURCE OF PROTEIN AND MAKE FOR THE FOUNDATION OF EVERY GOOD DIET. IF YOU DISLIKE THE TASTE, JUST ADD CHOCOLATE, BUTTER, FLOUR AND BAKE FOR 30 MINUTES.

RULE #16

ALWAYS TRAVEL WITH BACK UP EQUIPMENT

Stuff breaks. It's not a question of if, it's a matter of when. Shoe laces, mouth guards, chinstraps, cleat studs, face masks, gloves, strings, sticks, pads, a spare jersey and shorts. All types of equipment can and will break or malfunction at the most inopportune time. Plus I don't think there's a coach out there who hasn't had a player forget to pack something (usually a Juco transfer) which is yet another reason to carry a spare of everything. Remember Murphy's Law ... "Anything that can go wrong, will go wrong." (And usually at the most inopportune time.)

That law was created by Edward A. Murphy, Jr., a U.S. Air Force engineer. In 1947, Captain Murphy was involved in a rocket-sled experiment in which all 16 accelerator instruments were installed in the wrong way, which is precisely what resulted in Murphy's observation. I share that with you in case you thought you were having a "bad day".

RULE #17
NEVER $H!T
ON THE BUS TOILET

Self-Explanatory

RULE #18

IF YOU SLEEP UNTIL NOON YOU ONLY HAVE TO PAY FOR TWO MEALS INSTEAD OF THREE.

RULE #19
NEVER SIT
ON THE BUS TOILET

(This rule only applies to male travelers or since its 2019 travelers who identify as male. Sorry, didn't mean to assume anyone's gender.)

Guys, think about this... using the bathroom on a moving vehicle that is bouncing up and down and swaying back and forth is challenging at best. The odds of someone having perfect aim is about the same as the odds of winning the Powerball lottery. When your idiot goalie staggers into the bathroom drunk and half asleep at 2 am to take a leak, accuracy is the furthest thing from his mind.

*If you successfully follow rule #17, rule #19 should never be an issue.

RULE #20
NEVER TRUST ETHNIC RESTAURANTS WITH NON-ETHNIC NAMES

This is a life rule you should follow at all times, not just on the road with your team. Just like you never eat at a Chinese restaurant located next door to a pet store, never eat food at a strip club, never buy day old sushi marked "clearance" and never order "fresh seafood" in a land locked state.

A place named Billy Bob's Fine Italian Cuisine should be an immediate red flag. Just like Ed's Burrito Palace or Amy's Chinese Take-Out. At best you're not going to have a good meal, at worst you'll wind up with food poisoning and everyone will break rule #17 creating a new level of misery.

RULE #21

DON'T HAVE A VERY GOOD TEAM OR YOU'RE PLAYING A DIFFICULT OPPONENT?

TRY LAMINATING THE SCOUTING REPORT SO YOUR TEARS ROLL RIGHT OFF.

RULE #22
PLANES, TRAINS AND AUTOMOBILES

Sleep as much as humanly possible on whichever mode of transportation you're traveling in. If you're a coach, you're most likely a walking-talking study in sleep deprivation. Sleeping while traveling makes the road trip go by faster and helps you arrive feeling fresher whether you've changed time zones or not. It's a long season so you need to do everything you can to stay well rested. If it helps, don't think of it as napping or sleeping. Instead think of it as recovery, because that's a big part of what sleep really is.

RULE #23

ALWAYS TRAVEL WITH THE FOLLOWING SLEEP AIDS AND ACCESSORIES

- **Ear Plugs:** I'm a Division three coach so I use foam ear plugs because they're cheap and work good enough. If you're a division one coach you'll probably buy Bose noise-masking sleep buds. They only run $250 bucks. From what I understand Division two coaches stick headphones in their ears and just leave them unplugged.

- **Sleep mask:** Again, I'm a Division three coach so I use an old bandana as a blindfold. (Since I haven't had a raise in ten years, it also doubles as a handkerchief) If you're a division one coach, you'll probably want to purchase the Roama Travel Eye Mask. It's only $12,345.00 on Amazon so I'm sure it's easily within your budget.

- **A pillow or better yet a pillowcase:** Whether it's an inflatable neck pillow like you see for sale in airport gift shops or a regular pillow, comfort matters and having something soft to rest your head on helps. I recommend just a pillowcase not an actual pillow. If you're looking to save space bring a pillowcase instead. If you're ever in an emergency situation where you need a comfy pillow, just stuff some soft clothes in that case, lay your head down and snooze. Likewise, you can use the pillowcase to compress clothes like a puffy jacket in order to save space in your luggage. Our women's basketball coach at Radnor University just buys a box of wine and after she drinks it she fills the plastic bladder of it up with air to use as a pillow.

- **A blanket:** When you have a bus full of people it's impossible to have everyone agree on the same temperature. Plus in the fall and spring it's warm during the day and cold at night. Be part of the solution instead of the problem and just bring a blanket on board.

- **Medications:** I do not recommend the use of medication for sleep but to each his own. Some people take prescription Ambien others take over the counter sleep aids like Unisom or melatonin supplements. After a loss one of my three friends Johnny Walker, Jack Daniels or Jim Beam usually help me fall asleep.

- **Gadgets and Gizmos:** For those of you with nothing better to spend your money on (aka Division One coaches), you can get yourself an anxiety relieving sleep lamp, a self-cooling pillow, a wireless sound soother headband, a wake up light and sound machine from the Sharper Image catalog.

RULE #24

DOUBLE THE BATTERY LIFE OF YOUR IPHONE BY PUTTING THE DAMN THING DOWN EVERY NOW AND THEN.

RULE #25
TAKE THE SPORTS INFORMATION DIRECTOR SERIOUSLY...

...but don't take everything he says as gospel. SID's are complex creatures. What it boils down to is that they love their jobs but hate everyone involved with their jobs. They're responsible for how good you and your team look and sound to the media.

You're going to want to try and keep your SID as happy as possible. Be very careful not to do anything that in any way complicates or makes their job complicated or difficult in any way.

On the flip side, don't be too nice to your SID, they don't like that either. Sports Information Directors wield a lot of power. Power to make you look bad and they love nothing more than to make someone they dislike look bad.

RULE #26
NOBODY CARES

Nobody cares that you went to college for physical education or minored in coaching. You really don't want to ever bring this up because in some cases it will actually be held against you. Successful coaches who did major in physical education don't talk about it. *(Unless they attended Springfield College.)*

RULE #27
DO IT YOURSELF UNIVERSAL REMOTE.

Grab all your remotes in one hand and wrap a couple rubber bands around them. Boom.... Instant universal remote!! Now you can misplace all of them together instead of just one.

RULE #28
DON'T LIE ON YOUR RESUME

The coaching fraternity is a very small, tightly knit community where everyone knows everyone. If you only worked as an intern or graduate assistant you were not the associate head coach. The athletic directors reading your resume call references and perform background checks. The odds are they may even know your current employer personally. Don't lie about what degree you earned, who you worked for or your job title. It will come back to haunt you.

Case In Point: Let George O'Leary's employment as Notre Dame's head football coach serve as a cautionary tale. It lasted all of five days. That's how long it took Notre Dame officials to discover O'Leary lied about earning varsity letters in college when in fact he never even made it on to the field. He also lied about having a master's degree from SUNY-Stony Brook when in reality he attended but never graduated.

RULE #29
HOTEL CHECK OUT

Before you check out of the hotel, always take the little bottles of shampoo, conditioner and the small bars of soap with you as well as any extra rolls of toilet paper.

If you're a Division three coach this rule should be self-explanatory. If you're a Division one coach, you can afford quilted Charmin so ignore this rule.

RULE #30
DO IT YOURSELF TOOTH BRUSH HOLDER.

Buy a fountain drink at the convenience store, when you're done with it take the empty home, remove the straw from the plastic lid and replace it with your toothbrush.

RULE #31
THE 1% RULE

This rule is for all the unwanted people in your life. People like your athletic director, the booster club president, player's parents, NCAA investigators, the media and anyone else you'd prefer to avoid. When receiving a call from one of these people that you don't necessarily want to talk to but need to talk to, tell them at the beginning of the conversation that your phone is at 1% battery life and about to die. This way you are then free to hang up on them whenever you want without seeming rude.

RULE #32
THE ULTIMATE URBAN PARKING LIFE HACK

When recruiting in a major city like New York City or Chicago, to save on the ultra-high cost of public parking, find an auto repair or tire shop that has an inexpensive tire rotation deal. Have your tires rotated but tell them you have couple errands to run and can you come by and pick up the car later in the day.

RULE #33
DO IT YOURSELF WATER PROOF KEYBOARD.

Are you sick and tired of spilling coffee all over your keyboard like a savage? To avoid making a mess of your computer's keyboard while eating or drinking, just wrap saran wrap around it. You can still push all the buttons while keeping it clean and dry. Because God knows the IT department won't fix it in a timely manner and your athletic director has no money to replace your keyboard or buy you a new laptop. He's too busy buying himself important things like the newest iPhone for all the recruiting calls he doesn't make and the latest Mac Book Pro for all the emails he doesn't send.

RULE #34
DOCUMENTATION IS EVERYTHING

Take a picture of one of your tires when it's flat. Then the next time you want to skip an early morning athletic department staff meeting or bail on an after work event, send the picture to your boss and just enjoy your free time.

RULE #35
DIVISION ONE TRAVEL ON A DIVISION THREE BUDGET

When you're traveling by plane, dress professionally, be the very last person to board and if there's a seat open in first class sit there. Flight attendants rarely check boarding passes anymore so this easily should go undetected.

RULE #36
DO IT YOURSELF FLEECE VEST. CUT THE SLEEVES OFF YOUR FLEECE JACKET.

RULE #37
EARLY BOARDING

If you don't have the cojones to pull off rule #35 but don't want to wait until your zone boards do this. Tell the gate agent you have a peanut allergy and need to wipe down your seat. They will let you be one of the first people on the plane.

RULE #38
DON'T ASK THE FACILITIES MANAGER STUPID QUESTIONS.

Seriously, don't ask the facilities manager questions you should already know the answers to, questions he already answered or questions there are no answers for yet.

Being the facilities manager is a stressful enough job without getting bombarded with stupid questions from dozens of coaches daily. They are in season year round. They print facility schedules for everyone (or should) so that you will be up to date on all practice and game day information that is available to know. Before you ask a stupid question, check the facility calendar first. If the answer isn't there, you probably don't need to be asking the question. Excessive curiosity is a horrible habit to get into and will make him hate you almost as much as the sports information director does. So maybe ask the SID first.

RULE #39
MONEY SAVER

To save money, break up with your significant other before Christmas and get back together after Valentine's Day.

RULE #40
NEUTRAL SITE GAMES ARE NEVER A GOOD THING

If you're playing a neutral site game, you don't get any special treatment much less equitable treatment and you barely get a legit game in. There's no accountability when neither team is the host. What there will be is: limited use of locker rooms, the field will be painted wrong, may not even be regulation size, no press box access, and your complaints will be ignored.

RULE #41
LOW BUDGET AIR FRESHENERS

Scented Bounce dryer sheet are the poor man's air freshener. The most cost-effective way to prevent your equipment, travel bags, laundry bags and the entire bus from smelling like one big collective arm pit is to invest in a box of dryer sheets.

They are an amazing and convenient way to mask odors without smelling overwhelming themselves. Alternatively, just throw a bar of soap in with your dirty laundry (the mini soaps you steal from the hotel work great).

If you're a Division One coach disregard this rule. You probably either have a bus with built in air fresheners or charter a separate bus for transporting dirty laundry and stinky equipment.

RULE #42

KEEP CAKE MOIST BY EATING IT ALL IN ONE SITTING.

RULE #43
EARLY IS ON TIME,
ON TIME IS LATE,
LATE IS UNACCEPTABLE

Showing up late for a high school visit virtually guarantees you won't get a player from that coach's program. Coaches are repulsed by lateness. Plan ahead for traffic if you're visiting a major metropolitan area. Build in additional time to stop for gas, food and rest rooms. If you're smart, you'll make one stop at a place that has all three.

RULE #44
PACK AN EMPTY WATER BOTTLE TO TAKE TO THE AIRPORT

Is there any bigger racket in the world than a $5.00 bottle of water sold inside airports?

You'd have to be a Division One coach to be able to afford that. Pack an empty bottle so you can fill it up for free at the drinking fountain after you pass through security. I know some idiots freeze their water in a water bottle so it's not technically a liquid. And while that might work, do you really want to piss off the TSA agents who determine whether or not a passenger gets cavity searched? They hate you almost as much as your sports information director does.

Besides do you really want to awkwardly wait around for your water to melt when you're thirsty? Don't be a jackass, just pack an empty bottle.

RULE #45
PARK ANYWHERE FOR FREE.

To avoid getting costly parking tickets, just take the windshield wipers off of your car. Not just the wiper blade, but the whole arm as well. This will stop police from being able to give you a ticket, so you can park pretty much anywhere for as long as you'd like. To be safe, you better remove your license plate as well.

And your wheels, the cops can't boot a car with no wheels.

While you're at it, if you remove your entire car from the offending spot, you can also avoid tickets.

*Alternately, you could put a fake parking ticket under the wiper on your car. Then park wherever you want.

RULE #46
WRAP YOUR SHOES IN THE FREE HOTEL SHOWER CAP

You basically already paid for it along with the mini soaps and shampoos that you steal from the hotel, so you may as well take it. Wrapping your dirty shoes in it will keep the rest of your clothing clean in your suitcase. Conversely, wrapping your clean, freshly shined shoes in it will keep them from rubbing off on your other clothes in said suitcase.

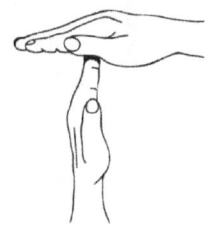

TIME OUT

We interrupt your regularly scheduled programming to bring you this important announcement about duct tape. Little do you know but duct tape is about to become the most valuable player in your program. Read rules #47-69 and it will revolutionize the way you solve problems. (You can thank me later.)

ALWAYS CARRY A ROLL OF DUCT TAPE

DUCT TAPE, IT'S LIKE A TOOL BOX ON A ROLL.

Duct tape was first invented in 1942 by Johnson & Johnson. It was designed to keep moisture out of ammunition cases. Since it has waterproof properties it was often referred to as "duck tape". Originally it was army green in color but after World War II its color was changed to grey because it became popular in the housing industry to connect heat and air conditioning ducts together. Hence the name "duct tape".

I'm pretty sure duct tape is what saved the entire Apollo 13 crew and I'm confident it will rescue you from disaster as well.

RULE #47
STRENGTH & CONDITIONING

To get stronger hold a large roll of duct tape out to your side by holding your arms parallel to the ground and keep holding them there until you can't any longer. Repeat with other arm.

RULE #48
REPLACEMENT LINT ROLLER

Wrap a piece around your hand and pat down your shirt and pants to remove the dirt, lint or fuzz that's wreaking havoc on your clothing.

RULE #49
CUP HOLDER

If your camp chair doesn't come with a cup holder, use your roll of duct tape to tape across the bottom of one end of the roll then tape the roll sideways to the arm of your chair. Now you have a cup holder.

RULE #50
FIRST AID

If you ever get a blister on your foot and you don't have any band aids left in the medical kit, use a piece of duct tape. Slap a little cotton gauze over it then tape your blister with the duct tape, the non-sticky side is slippery and it won't cause friction on the blistered area.

RULE #51
I'M AFRAID NOT OR IS IT I'M A FRAYED KNOT?

If the plastic tips of your shoe laces begin to crack or break wrap a small piece of duct tape around them. Problem solved.

RULE #52
FIX A DAMAGED WATER BOTTLE

A cracked Gatorade bottle can be a serious problem (and if you're a Division 3 coach, an expensive proposition). Apply the tape to the water bottle when it is completely dry otherwise it won't stick well. This will prevent leaking when you refill it. And if your Athletic Director is as cheap as mine, he will refuse to buy replacement bottles. So you should do what I do the beginning of every season and wrap your bottles with duct tape to begin with as a protective measure.

RULE #53
PATCH A HOSE

Share this tip with your grounds crew. You can use duct tape to temporarily patch cuts or holes in garden hoses. It's not a permanent fix but it will get you through just long enough to convince your athletic director he needs to buy a new hose for the field.

RULE #54
GOT A SPLINTER?

Share this one with your athletic trainer. Because duct tape is so incredibly sticky it's great at removing small splinters. If you can't find tweezers in the medical kit or training room just stick a piece of duct tape over the area where your splinter is. Slowly peel the tape off. If it doesn't come out right away on the first try repeat until it is removed.

*Important Detail: Pull the tape the opposite direction of the splinter entry.

RULE #55
FLY CATCHER

If you've got a ton of flies in the office, locker room, dug out, equipment shed or anywhere else and your athletic director is too cheap to buy fly paper grab your roll of duct tape. Hang a long piece of duct tape up and it will do essentially the same job as actual fly paper. The flies are attracted to the scent of the adhesive glue on the tape.

*Also works on crickets and other types of bugs you might find in your basement.

RULE #56
GOT WARTS?

Duct tape can cover up ugly stuff you need to repair and it's also great at getting rid of ugly stuff that clings to your body. Like warts! According to Web MD (which is where I get all my medical advice) duct tape proved more effective at treating warts than having them frozen off.

Cover the wart with duct tape and leave the tape on for at least a week. If the tape falls off, replace it immediately. If the wart is still there put a fresh piece of tape on it and repeat weekly until it's gone. If this works for you, you're officially the second coming of MacGyver.

*Note: Not for use on genitals. Different kind of warts.

RULE #57
CHIPS

If you're one of those freakishly self-disciplined people who can resist eating an entire bag of potato chips in one sitting, first of all—congratulations, you're officially a much better person than I am. Secondly, you can use a piece of duct tape to seal the bag of chips shut and make sure your chips don't get stale. Just fold the top of the bag over and seal it shut.

RULE #58
DIY MOUSEPAD

If you're a small college coach like me, you probably can't afford an actual mousepad. You can make your own by completely covering a square piece of cardboard with strips of duct tape. If you're a Division One coach and are reading this, please send me an actual mousepad. I'd gladly accept your donation. It will go nicely with my computer that hasn't been upgraded since the Reagan administration was in office.

RULE #59
TAPE YOUR VCR SHUT

If your video tapes in your video cassette recorder won't stay in the VCR, duct tape it closed so that you can finish watching your game film.

RULE #60
PRODUCTIVITY TOOL

Duct tape your assistant coaches hand to their phone to keep them from taking too many breaks when making recruiting calls.

RULE #61
CHEAPER THAN
POST-IT™ NOTES

Who needs to spend money you don't have in your budget on Post-It Notes when you can make your own self-sticking notes with a piece of paper and some duct tape.

RULE #62

DIVISION THREE INTER-OFFICE COMMUNICATION

When the phone system goes down, attach two tin cans with long strips of duct tape.

*Don't call the Sports Information Director though, remember he already hates you.

RULE #63
RECRUITING THAT STICKS

Place duct tape, sticky-side-out, on your media guides so recruits find them hard to put down.

RULE #64
OFFICE HUMOR

Tape the backs of desk drawers to the back of the Sports Information Director's desk and his filing cabinets so they won't open. Why not, he already hates you.

RULE #65

FORGET POSTSEASON, HOW ABOUT DEER SEASON

"Borrow" (steal) the athletic trainer's golf cart and cover it with camo duct tape to turn it into a portable deer blind during hunting season.

RULE #66
EASY TO I.D. LUGGAGE

Wrap a strip of bright colored duct tape around your luggage when you're flying. This will make your suitcase easy to identify and also help keep it closed when baggage handlers are throwing it onto and off of the airplanes.

*Bonus: You'll also know if it was tampered with if you see it's been torn when you retrieve your suitcase at baggage claim.

RULE #67
SICK OF READING THIS?

Put the book down for the day, fold a foot long piece of duct tape in half and you just make yourself bookmark. Besides, if you're a small college coach like me, you probably can't afford to buy an actual bookmark anyway.

RULE #68
INSULATION

Duct tape makes a great insulator for drinks. Wrap your beer can or bottle in duct tape to keep it cold longer. Plus no one will see you're drinking a beer at a school function.

RULE #69
VERSATILITY

Duct tape can fix a lot of things. The one thing it can't do is fix stupid, but it can muffle the sound.

*We now resume your regularly scheduled programming.

(Oh and you're welcome.)

RULE #70
THE BEAR TACTIC.

When flying Southwest Airlines which has no assigned seating, utilize what I call The Bear Tactic. Just like when you encounter a bear in the woods, make yourself as big as possible to scare away anyone who might think about sitting next to you. If the flight isn't completely full, you'll at least keep one seat vacant next to you. If you pull your pants down to your ankles you'll probably get the entire row to yourself.

RULE #71

DON'T SPEND TOO MUCH MONEY ON YOUR SPOUSE BY NOT HAVING ONE.

RULE #72
SAVE MONEY ON PARKING.

At public lots or garages, walk back to your car through the vehicle entrance, grab new ticket, then leave for free.

RULE #73
CHECKED BAGGAGE

If you have to check baggage (of the non-emotional variety) because you're going to be away for days on end mark your bag as "fragile". It causes the 'throwers' (baggage handlers) to treat it more carefully, and elevates your bag to the top of the trolley, meaning it will hit the carousel quicker (sometimes yours is the first bag out!)

RULE #74
FINANCIAL INTELLIGENCE

Teach your players about taxes by taking 20% of their meal money from them on road trips.

RULE #75
NEVER LEAVE A PAPER TRAIL

Always have alcoholic beverages put on a separate check. DO NOT attempt to pay for cocktails using the school credit card. Refer to rule #74 and pay cash for the bar tab with the meal money you withheld from your players.

Business managers LOVE to get coaches in trouble with the administration over this very issue so don't leave any evidence in the form of a credit card receipt with eight pitchers of beer from Hooters on it.

RULE #76
REFER BACK TO RULE #75

If you were dumb enough to break rule #75 even if you convinced the stripper errr waitress to separate the alcohol from the food DO NOT attempt to expense a meal from anywhere with a name like: The Booby Trap, Bottoms Up, The Rear End, Teasers, Assets, Show-n-Tail, Mammary Lane, The Landing Strip, Bare Essentials, Treasure Chest, The Lusty Leopard, Dangerous Curves, The Body Shop, Twin Peaks, Cheatahs, Scuttlebutt, The Eager Beaver, or Shot Gun Willies.

(And YES this is indeed a lesson I learned the hard way when I returned from a recruiting trip and accidentally submitted a receipt from Starbutts.)

RULE #77

THE TRICK TO NOT CRYING WHEN YOU CUT ONIONS IS TO NOT FORM AN EMOTIONAL CONNECTION TO THE ONION.

RULE #78
TRUST BUT VERIFY.

If you think a prospect might be giving you an incorrect cell phone number to get rid of you, read it back to them incorrectly. If they correct you, it's legit.

*Guys, this same strategy works with girls you're trying to flirt with.

RULE #79

IF YOU'RE AN ASSISTANT COACH AVOID COMPLAINING

If you're an assistant the benefits, incentives and perks that go with your job are probably minimal compared to your head coach. He or she will get all the credit and you will probably do much of the work. Deal with it, that's just the way it is, has always been and that dynamic probably won't change any time soon.

If you work hard enough and last long enough one day you'll either become a head coach yourself or your genius will be recognized. Until then be grateful for the position you're in even if you have to fake it and never complain about or bad mouth your head coach in public or private.

RULE #80

FITNESS TIP: WHEN YOU ARRIVE AT WORK, PARK IN THE FARTHEST SPOT FROM THE OFFICE, THEN PUSH YOUR CAR TO A CLOSER SPOT.

RULE #81

ASSISTANT COACHES: EXCUSES ARE LIKE A CAR WITHOUT AN ENGINE.

They get you nowhere. You shouldn't complain about things outside your control and even if you do complain about things within your control guess what... you'll be the one selected to fix it. Just take the initiative to make whatever situation you want to complain about better without complaining about it.

I remember I complained about how poor the budget was at my first assistant coaching job about five minutes later the head coach put me in charge of fundraising. A couple years ago my assistant coach complained about the box lunches. It became contagious, next thing you know most of the team was bitching and moaning about the sandwiches. I put that assistant in charge of making everybody's sandwiches to order instead of simply having the cafeteria prepared four dozen ham and cheese sandwiches.

So let this be a lesson to be careful about what you complain about.

RULE #82
WHAT'S IN A NAME?

Never hire an assistant coach or recruit players who attended high school anywhere with Country Day, Prep or Academy in the name. They tend to complain about box lunches.
Just an observation.

RULE #83

IF YOU PUT TOO MUCH SALSA ON YOUR TORTILLA CHIP JUST PUT ANOTHER CHIP IN YOUR MOUTH TO BALANCE IT OUT.

BONUS RULE #84
FITNESS TIP:

Train your core by pulling the dining room table to you instead of pulling your chair to the table.

RULE #85

VISITING TEAM LOCKER ROOMS COME IN ALL SHAPES AND SIZES

You'd be shocked at what some schools call the "visiting team locker room". Visitor locker rooms are usually cramped spaces that are not meant to be comfortable for the opponent. Perhaps the most famous example of this is the University of Iowa's Kinnick Stadium visiting team locker room. Former football coach Hayden Fry once read that the color pink can have a calming effect on people. So in 1979 he ordered the walls and floor in the visitors' locker room to be painted pink. In 2005 pink lockers, showers, towels and toilets were also added.

Expect cold showers, cramped quarters and bad odors. It all comes with the territory. One team on our schedule, which will remain nameless, houses the visitor's locker room a half mile walk away from the game field and there's no road to take you by bus from the locker room to the field.

Just go ahead and plan on your team using the bus as a dressing room for all away games. Anything nicer is just a bonus.

RULE #86
GENTLEMEN

It's a well-known fact that telling your wife to calm down will only make her more upset. Instead, I recommend you try to make her angrier, which will help her relax. I suggest telling her to calm down.

RULE #87

PLAN ON SELLING OR TRADING IN YOUR CAR?

DRIVE IT IN REVERSE FOR A MONTH OR TWO TO LOWER THE MILEAGE.

RULE #88
BATTERY LIFE

Save the battery life on your phone by not turning it on. Seriously. Especially not at practice, nothing says "you're just not that important" to your players quite like taking phone calls or texting during practice. *(Unless of course it's a recruit better than anyone currently on your roster, then of course talk to them or text all you want.)*

RULE #89

AKA #DIVISION3PROBLEMS

IF YOU CAN'T AFFORD COASTERS, USE FREE CARPET SAMPLES FROM HOME DEPOT OR LOWES.

RANDALL'S RULES VOLUME ONE

RULE #90
SAVE MONEY

Let your health problems build up and cover them all in one doctor's appointment.

RULE #91

ICE CREAM TOO FROZEN TO SCOOP?

MICROWAVE YOUR SPOON FOR 30 SECONDS.

RULE #92
HEALTH TIP

Find a doctor younger than you.
You can't live to 100 if your doctor dies before you do.

FINAL THOUGHTS

If you have to sneak it to do it, lie to cover it up, or delete it to avoid being seen, then you probably shouldn't be doing it to begin with.

ABOUT THE AUTHOR

Morgan Randall is a great American philosopher, coach, mentor and legend (in his own mind). He has been leading teams at Radnor University for over forty years and has no plans on retiring any time soon. In 2012 the Radnor University administration awarded him a lifetime contract. It's the only award he has ever wanted.

While he has hundreds of wins to his credit, Coach Randall is a member of zero halls of fame and has no interest in belonging to any organization that would have him as a member. According to Randall *"coaching is about the rewards not the awards and the rewards are in the relationships"*.

More information is available at: **CoachMorganRandall.com**

OTHER BOOKS BY COACH RANDALL

If you've enjoyed reading *Randall's Rules volume one* you will also love *Randall's Rules volume two and* the many other books in the Participation Trophy Book series by Coach Morgan Randall. More information is available at:
ParticipationTrophyBooks.com

If you've enjoyed reading *Randall's Rules* you will also love the many other books in the Participation Trophy Book series by Coach Morgan Randall. More information is available at: **ParticipationTrophyBooks.com**

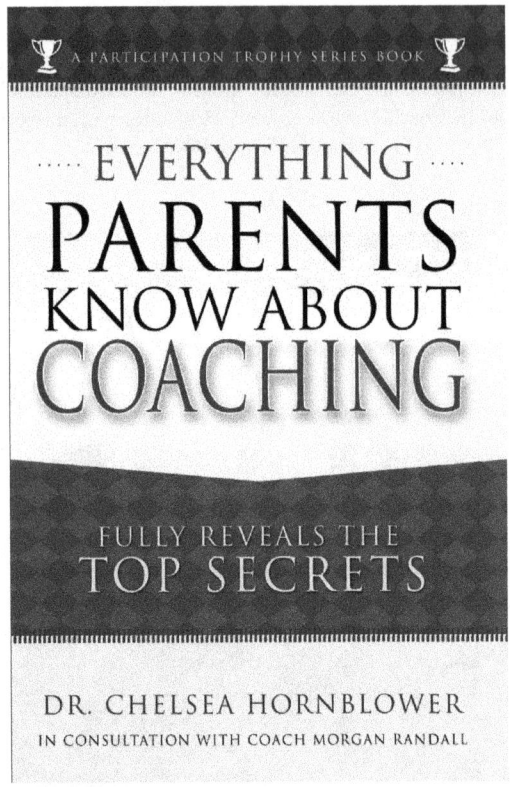

COACH MORGAN RANDALL

Do your players have an uncontrollable urge to sleep through practice? Do they sometimes struggle to find the motivation to attend practice?

If so, they may be suffering from a condition known as EPA or Excessive Practice Absence. These symptoms also coincide with: difficulty holding yourself accountable, not understanding your role and shirking responsibilities on your team. For help treating their case of EPA buy this book and also go to:
AccountabilityIssues.com

www.ingramcontent.com/pod-product-compliance
Lightning Source LLC
Chambersburg PA
CBHW070928160426
43193CB00011B/1607